F U N
with
FELT

FUN
with
FELT

LYN ORTON

GOLDEN

A GOLDEN BOOK®

Western Publishing Company Inc, Racine, Wisconsin 53404

GOLDEN®, GOLDEN & DESIGN®, A GOLDEN BOOK®, AND A LITTLE GOLDEN BOOK®
are registered trademarks of Western Publishing Company Inc.
Published by Western Publishing Company Inc,
25-31 Tavistock Place, London WC1H 9SU.

© Salamander Books Ltd, 1994
129-137 York Way,
London N7 9LG,
United Kingdom.

ISBN 0-307-80810-6

CREDITS

Editor: Jilly Glassborow

Designer: Patrick Knowles

Photographers: Mark Gatehouse and Jonathan Pollock

Craft adviser: Leslie Thompson

Typeset by: SX Composing Ltd., Rayleigh, Essex

Colour separation by: Scantrans Pte. Ltd., Singapore

Printed in Belgium by: Proost International Book Production

Contents

INTRODUCTION

There are so many exciting things to make with felt, and a rainbow of wonderful colours to choose from too! Unlike many materials, felt is easy to cut into crisp shapes, with edges that won't fray, and it can be sewn or glued to make all kinds of designs. When having fun with felt, play safe. Don't leave scissors lying open and always store needles and pins in a pin cushion or felt square when you're not using them.

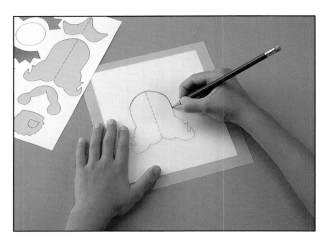

Making a Pattern For large shapes, trace the pattern at the back of this book and cut it out. For smaller shapes, make a template by laying your trace face down on to card and redrawing over the outline so the shape appears on the card. Cut it out.

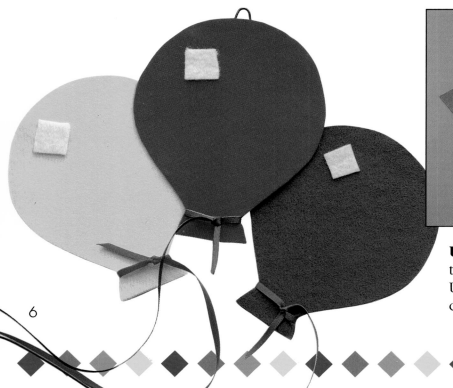

Using a Pattern Pin your paper pattern on to the felt, keeping it as flat as possible. Using the edge of the paper as a guide, carefully cut out your shape.

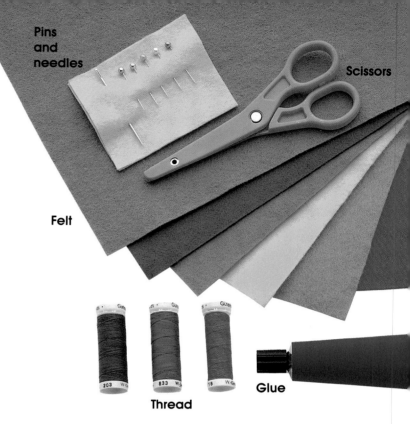

Using a Template Lay your card shape on to the felt and draw round it using a ball-point pen. Don't use a felt-tip pen as the ink may spread. Now cut the felt shape out.

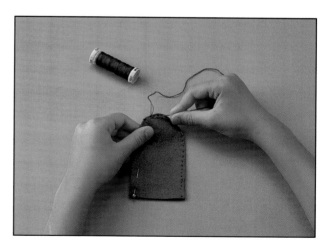

Sticking With Glue Always use a fabric or all-purpose glue to stick felt together. You only need a small amount, as too much may soak through the fabric and stain it. Never allow the felt to get wet as it will lose its shape and colour.

Sewing Felt There is no need to hem felt as it doesn't fray. Carefully pin the pieces into position and sew small neat stitches close to the edge.

7

Pig on a Stick

Test your sewing skills with these comic stick puppets. If you don't like sewing, you can glue the head together instead.

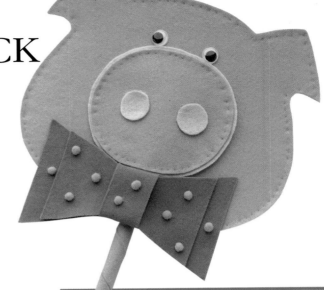

You will need

(for each pig)
Two squares of pink felt
Beige felt
Coloured felt for bow
Craft interfacing
Pair of joggle eyes
Small coloured pompoms
40cm (15in) of wooden dowel
Tracing paper and pencil
Needle and pins
Matching thread
Scissors
All-purpose glue

1 Trace the head pattern on page 28. Turn your trace over along the dotted line and finish off the other half. Now trace the other pattern pieces. Trace the snout and the bow twice, following the dotted lines for the second trace.

2 Cut out all the pattern pieces and pin them on to coloured felt. Cut out all the felt shapes. Also cut out two felt circles about 2cm (¾in) across for the nostrils. Now cut out the head shape from craft interfacing. Pin the felt head on to the interfacing head and neatly sew all round the edge.

3 Pin and sew the pink and beige snouts together. Glue the snout on to the head, then stick the nostrils and joggle eyes in place.

4 Cut long strips of pink felt 15mm (½in) wide. Glue the end of one strip to the top of the dowel. Wind the felt round the stick, gluing it in place as you go. Finish covering the stick with felt, then glue it to the pig's head.

5 Place the small bow on top of the large one. Wrap the felt strip round the middle and glue it at the back. Then glue the bow tie to the piggy and decorate it with pompoms.

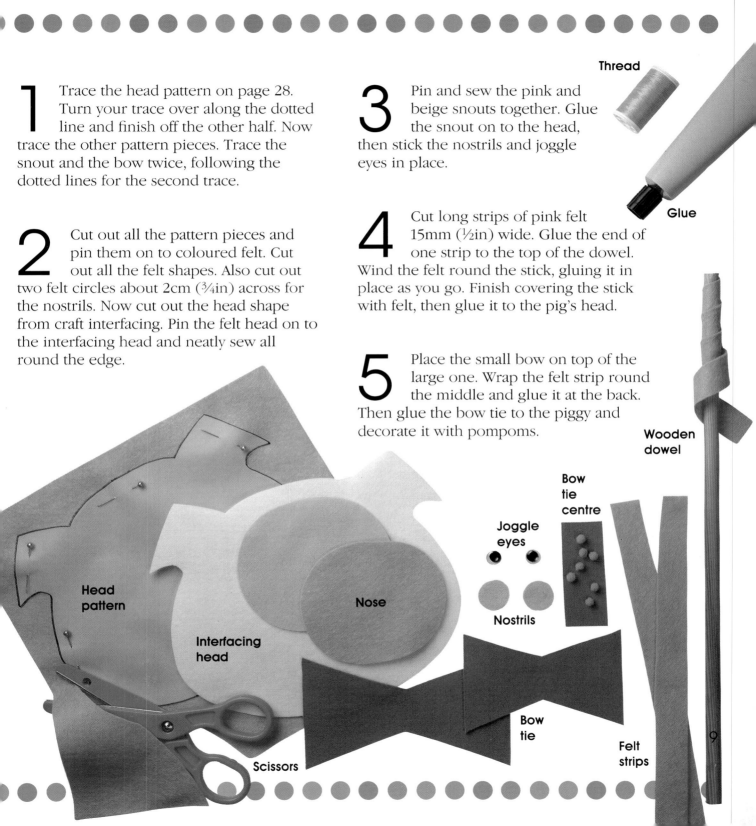

Thread

Glue

Wooden dowel

Bow tie centre

Joggle eyes

Nostrils

Head pattern

Interfacing head

Nose

Bow tie

Scissors

Felt strips

9

Flying High

Make these colourful high-flying aeroplanes to decorate your bedroom. If you want to make them different sizes, ask an adult to change the size of the pattern on a photocopier.

You will need

(for each aeroplane)
Different coloured felt
1 small joggle eye
1 pompom
1m (1yd) of narrow ribbon
Tracing paper and pencil
White card
Coloured card
Ball-point pen
Scissors
All-purpose glue

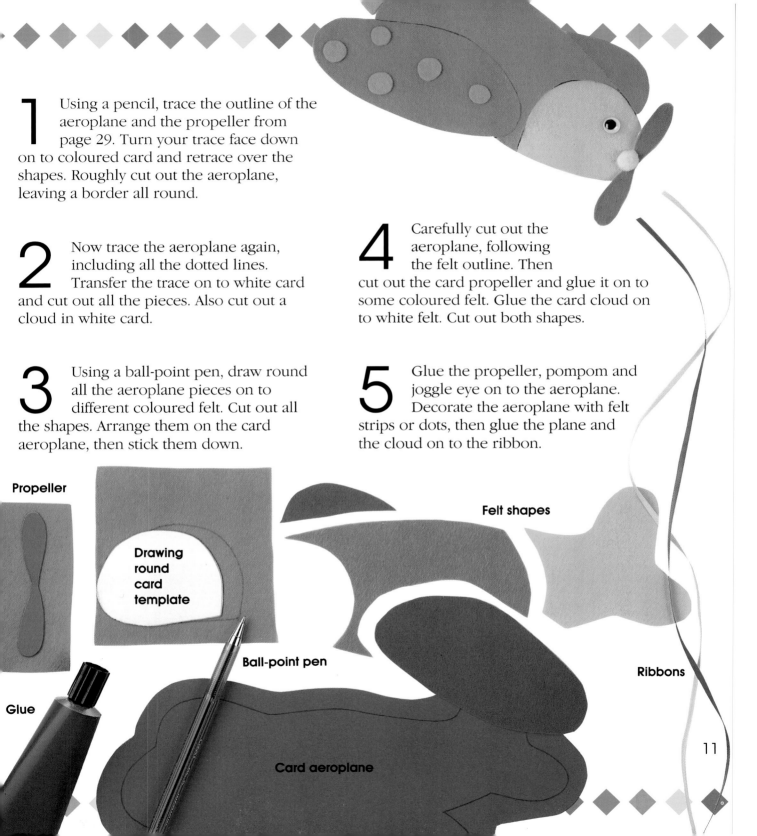

1 Using a pencil, trace the outline of the aeroplane and the propeller from page 29. Turn your trace face down on to coloured card and retrace over the shapes. Roughly cut out the aeroplane, leaving a border all round.

2 Now trace the aeroplane again, including all the dotted lines. Transfer the trace on to white card and cut out all the pieces. Also cut out a cloud in white card.

3 Using a ball-point pen, draw round all the aeroplane pieces on to different coloured felt. Cut out all the shapes. Arrange them on the card aeroplane, then stick them down.

4 Carefully cut out the aeroplane, following the felt outline. Then cut out the card propeller and glue it on to some coloured felt. Glue the card cloud on to white felt. Cut out both shapes.

5 Glue the propeller, pompom and joggle eye on to the aeroplane. Decorate the aeroplane with felt strips or dots, then glue the plane and the cloud on to the ribbon.

Propeller

Drawing round card template

Felt shapes

Ball-point pen

Ribbons

Glue

Card aeroplane

11

SPIDERS AND FLIES

Make this fun felt game to play with a friend. You play it just like noughts and crosses. And just in case you don't know how to play this, we tell you how on the next page.

YOU WILL NEED

20cm (8in) square of yellow felt
Green felt
Scraps of red, dark blue and
    pale blue felt
Tracing paper and pencil
White card
Ball-point pen
15 small joggle eyes
    Scissors
        All-purpose glue

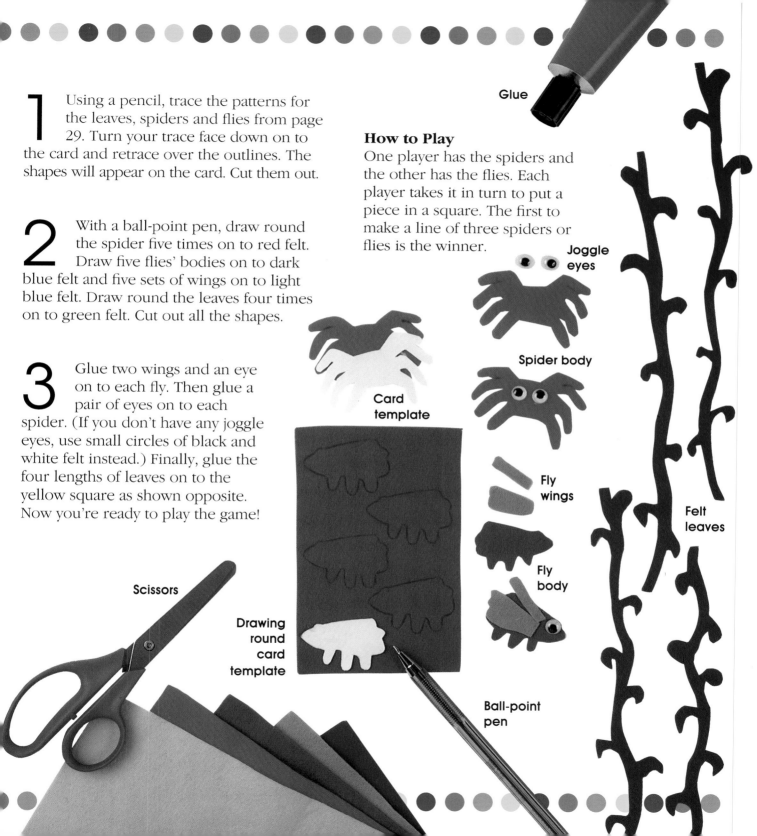

1 Using a pencil, trace the patterns for the leaves, spiders and flies from page 29. Turn your trace face down on to the card and retrace over the outlines. The shapes will appear on the card. Cut them out.

2 With a ball-point pen, draw round the spider five times on to red felt. Draw five flies' bodies on to dark blue felt and five sets of wings on to light blue felt. Draw round the leaves four times on to green felt. Cut out all the shapes.

3 Glue two wings and an eye on to each fly. Then glue a pair of eyes on to each spider. (If you don't have any joggle eyes, use small circles of black and white felt instead.) Finally, glue the four lengths of leaves on to the yellow square as shown opposite. Now you're ready to play the game!

How to Play
One player has the spiders and the other has the flies. Each player takes it in turn to put a piece in a square. The first to make a line of three spiders or flies is the winner.

Glue

Joggle eyes

Spider body

Card template

Fly wings

Fly body

Felt leaves

Scissors

Drawing round card template

Ball-point pen

BEAUTIFUL BALLOONS

These colourful balloons look great hung on the wall or in front of a window. Or why not make them to stick on a birthday card or party invitation? We show you how to make your own cards on page 18.

cards on page 18.

YOU WILL NEED

Red, blue and yellow felt
Scraps of white felt
1m (1yd) each of narrow red,
    blue and green ribbon
Tracing paper and pencil
White card
Sticky-backed paper hook
Scissors
All-purpose glue

1 Using a pencil, trace the pattern for the balloon from page 29. Turn your trace face down on to a piece of card and retrace over the outline. The shape will appear on the card. Cut out a square around the balloon shape, but do not cut the balloon out yet.

2 Glue the back of your card on to some coloured felt. When the glue has dried, cut out the balloon shape, as shown below, through both thicknesses. Now make two more coloured balloons in the same way.

3 If you want to hang your balloons in a window, you can also cover the backs in felt at this stage. Now glue the three balloons together so that they overlap as shown opposite. Cut out three small squares of white felt and glue them on to the balloons to make them shine.

4 Tie a length of ribbon to the neck of each balloon, finishing off with a bow. Finally, stick the paper hook on to the back of your balloons, at the top, so that you can hang your balloons up.

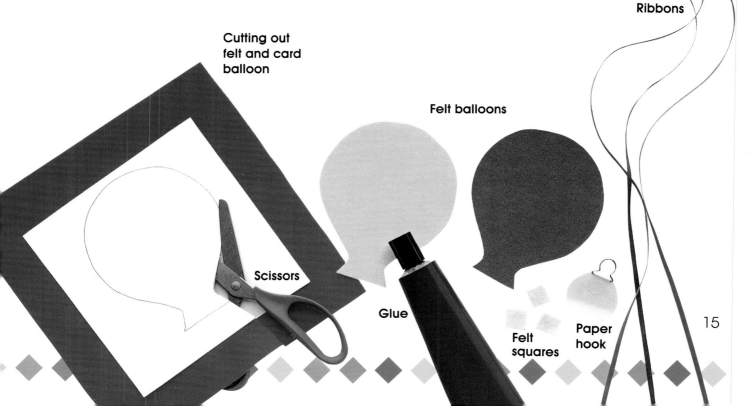

Cutting out felt and card balloon

Felt balloons

Ribbons

Scissors

Glue

Felt squares

Paper hook

15

ICE CREAM PIN CUSHIONS

These scrumptious ice creams will never melt! And they make the perfect gift for someone who enjoys sewing. Make them any size you like – the pattern is so simple you can easily draw it larger or smaller.

1 Trace the pattern for the cone shape from page 30. Cut out the tracing and pin it on to the felt. Cut out the felt shape. Now pin the pattern on to the wadding and cut out a wadding cone.

2 Place the wadding and the felt cones together. Thread a darning needle with embroidery thread and sew several rows of long stitches across the cone as shown below, through both layers.

3 Fold the cone shape in half, with the straight edges together and the wadding on the outside. Pin the straight edges together, then sew neatly close to the edge with ordinary thread. Leave the long curved end open.

4 Carefully turn the cone the right way out. Use a pencil to help you poke out the pointed end of the cone.

5 Scrunch up some polyester filling and stuff it into the cone until it is firmly packed. Leave some filling popping out of the top to look like ice cream. Lightly glue the filling to the inside of the cone to hold it in place.

6 Finally, glue coloured pompoms to the top of the wadding. If you haven't got any pompoms, use circles of coloured felt instead.

Glue

Embroidery thread

Pompoms

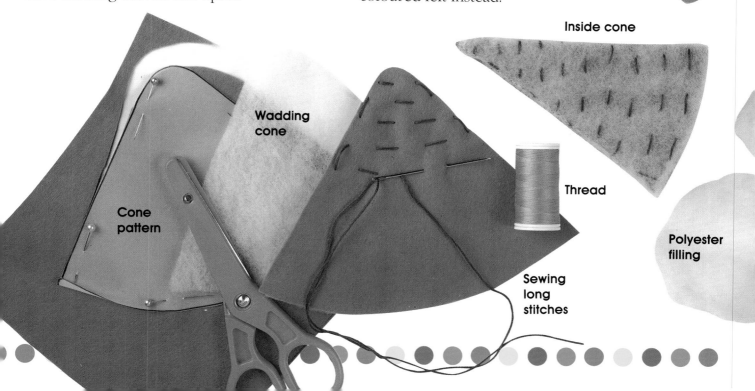

Inside cone

Wadding cone

Thread

Cone pattern

Sewing long stitches

Polyester filling

MIXED GREETINGS

It's great fun to make your own greeting cards. You can either copy the designs shown here or make up some of your own. We give you the measurements for the large card, but you can make your card any size you like.

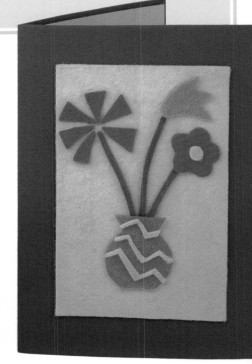

1 Cut a rectangle of coloured card 23cm × 15cm (9in × 6in). Using a ruler, draw a line widthways down the centre of the card. Then 'draw' down this line using a knitting needle to crease, or score, the paper. Fold the card in half.

2 Open out the card and cover the outside with glue. Stick the card on to a large piece of cotton fabric and smooth the fabric down flat. Cut away the extra fabric, leaving a 15mm (½in) border all around the card.

3 Cut away the corners of the fabric as shown below. Then glue the borders on to the inside of the card. When the glue is dry, refold the card.

4 Cut a rectangle of felt 11.5cm × 7.5cm (4½in × 3in). Glue it on to the front of the card, making sure that the card opens the right way.

5 Now draw a pattern for your design on to plain card. You can either copy our designs or make up your own, experimenting first on scraps of paper. Cut out all the shapes and draw round them on to coloured felt. Then cut out the felt shapes and glue them on to the front of the greeting card.

6 Cut two pieces of coloured card 14.5cm × 11cm (5¾in × 4¼in) and glue them inside your card so that they cover the edges of the fabric. Now you can write your message. You could even try making a coloured envelope as well.

Inside card

Felt shapes

Glue

Felt rectangle

Scissors

Card for lining inside

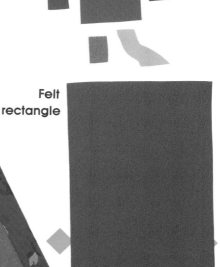

Spotted Ladybirds

If you enjoy sewing you'll love making these jolly ladybirds. They make charming presents and, because they double up as pin cushions, you can even give one to an adult. They are quite complicated to make so follow the instructions carefully. Begin by tracing the patterns from page 30 using a pencil.

tracing the patterns from page 30

You will need

(for each ladybird)

Black felt

Red or yellow felt

Polyester wadding

Pair of small joggle eyes

3 black chenille pipe cleaners

Tracing paper and pencil

Needle and pins

Matching thread

Scissors

All-purpose glue

1 Cut out the tracings and pin the body pattern on to some red or yellow felt. Cut out the shape. Then use the pattern to cut out two more body pieces. Pin the pattern for the base and head on to black felt. Cut out the shapes.

2 Pin the three body pieces together as shown. Neatly sew along both seams about 5mm (¼in) from the edge.

3 Open out the body and pin it on to the black felt base, keeping the seams outermost. Neatly sew the body on to the base, leaving a gap at one end so you can turn and stuff your ladybird.

4 Turn the ladybird the right way out through the gap. Stuff it with wadding until it is nice and fat. Then pin the black head on to the open end, covering up the gap as you do so. Sew the head neatly in place.

5 Cut a long narrow strip out of black felt and some black spots. Glue them on to the ladybird's back, trimming the strip as necessary.

6 To make the legs, cut two pipe cleaners down to 15cm (6in) and the other to 17.5cm (7in). Bend them at the knees and ankles as shown and glue them on to the base of the ladybird, putting the longer one in the middle.

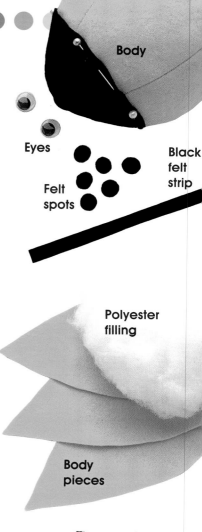

Glue

Body

Eyes

Felt spots

Black felt strip

Polyester filling

Body pieces

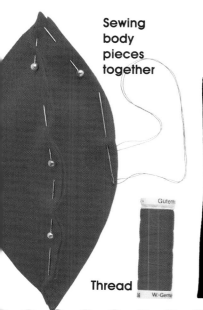

Sewing body pieces together

Thread

Head pattern

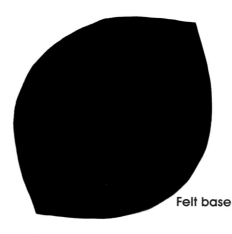

Felt base

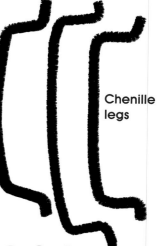

Chenille legs

ROYAL FINGER PUPPETS

These fun finger puppets are quite fiddly to make, but they're well worth the effort. Once you've made them, you could make up your own play about them.

YOU WILL NEED

Scraps of different
    coloured felt
Small joggle eyes
Small bells (for jester)
Gold stars
Narrow ribbon
Small red and yellow pompoms
Thread to match body colour
Tracing paper and pencil
White card
Ball-point pen
Needle and pins
Scissors
All-purpose glue

King

Queen

Jester

Princess

22

1 Decide which puppet you are going to make, then trace the patterns from page 31 using a pencil. Turn your trace face down on to some card and retrace over the outlines. Cut out all the shapes.

2 Glue the crown on to yellow felt to stiffen it. Then draw round the other card shapes on to different coloured felt. You will need to draw two of some shapes, such as the body, feet and sleeves. Cut out all the felt shapes.

3 Pin the two body pieces together. Then neatly sew all round, close to the edge. Leave the bottom edge open.

4 Arrange all the pieces on the body, then glue them in place. Stick the jester's hat on to the card template to stiffen it before you glue it on to his head.

5 Stick a small red pompom or felt dot in place for the nose. Cut a heart shaped mouth for the queen and princess, and a moustache for the king. Finally, decorate the puppets with gold stars, bells and pompoms.

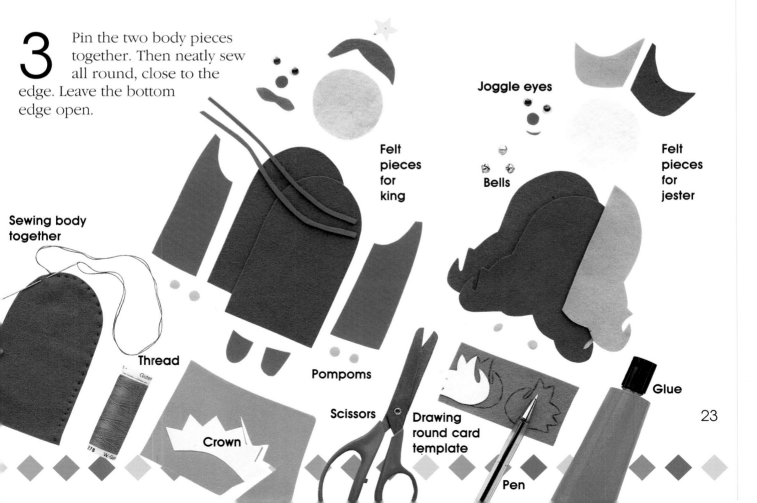

Joggle eyes

Felt pieces for king

Bells

Felt pieces for jester

Sewing body together

Thread

Pompoms

Scissors

Drawing round card template

Crown

Glue

Pen

23

FUN FELT BAG

This colourful, sixties-style bag is great fun for carrying your books to school. It also makes an ideal beach bag. You will find patterns for the flowers on page 32. Begin by cutting a rectangle of felt 75cm × 30cm (30in × 12in).

YOU WILL NEED

Large piece of felt
Squares of felt in various
    colours
40 or so small pompoms
White card
Tracing paper and pencil
Ball-point pen
Pins, needle and thread
Scissors
All-purpose glue

Thread

Needle

Glass-headed pins

Card flower template

Pompoms

Scissors

1 Cut two strips of felt measuring 3cm × 30cm (1in × 12in) off the end of the felt rectangle. These are your bag handles.

2 Fold one of the handles into a U-shape and pin it on to one short end of the felt rectangle. Now pin the second handle to the opposite end. Sew the handles in place.

3 Fold the bag in half, matching the short ends. Pin the sides together, then sew them together about 1cm (½in) from the edge.

4 Trace the three flower shapes from page 32. Turn your trace face down on to the card and retrace over the outlines. Cut out the card shapes. Draw round the shapes on to the felt squares using a ball-point pen. Cut out lots of different coloured flowers.

5 Arrange the felt flower shapes on to your bag and glue them in place. Decorate the centre of the flowers with the felt circles and pompoms.

FLOWER BROOCHES

These jolly flower brooches are very easy to make and will brighten up any outfit. You will need squares of felt in six bright colours – either copy the colours we have chosen or make up your own colour schemes. The patterns for the brooches are shown in pink on page 32. Start by tracing them off the page, using a pencil. Trace the large, round petalled flower and the large flower centre twice.

YOU WILL NEED

Scissors
Tracing paper and pencil
White card
3 safety pins
Needle and thread
All-purpose glue
6 small joggle eyes
6 squares of coloured felt

Scissors

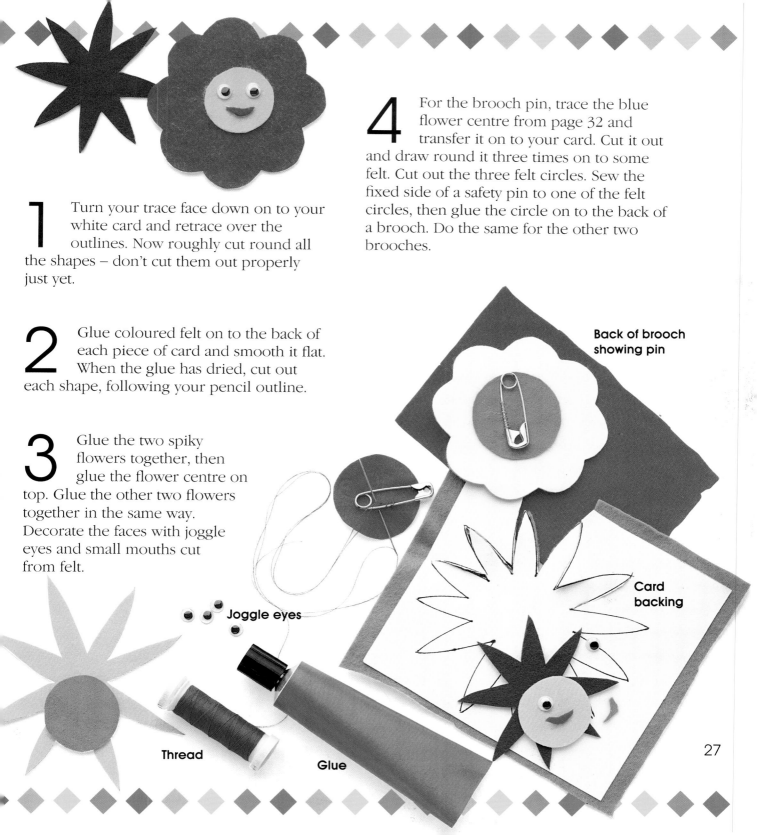

1 Turn your trace face down on to your white card and retrace over the outlines. Now roughly cut round all the shapes – don't cut them out properly just yet.

2 Glue coloured felt on to the back of each piece of card and smooth it flat. When the glue has dried, cut out each shape, following your pencil outline.

3 Glue the two spiky flowers together, then glue the flower centre on top. Glue the other two flowers together in the same way. Decorate the faces with joggle eyes and small mouths cut from felt.

4 For the brooch pin, trace the blue flower centre from page 32 and transfer it on to your card. Cut it out and draw round it three times on to some felt. Cut out the three felt circles. Sew the fixed side of a safety pin to one of the felt circles, then glue the circle on to the back of a brooch. Do the same for the other two brooches.

Back of brooch showing pin

Card backing

Joggle eyes

Thread

Glue

PATTERNS

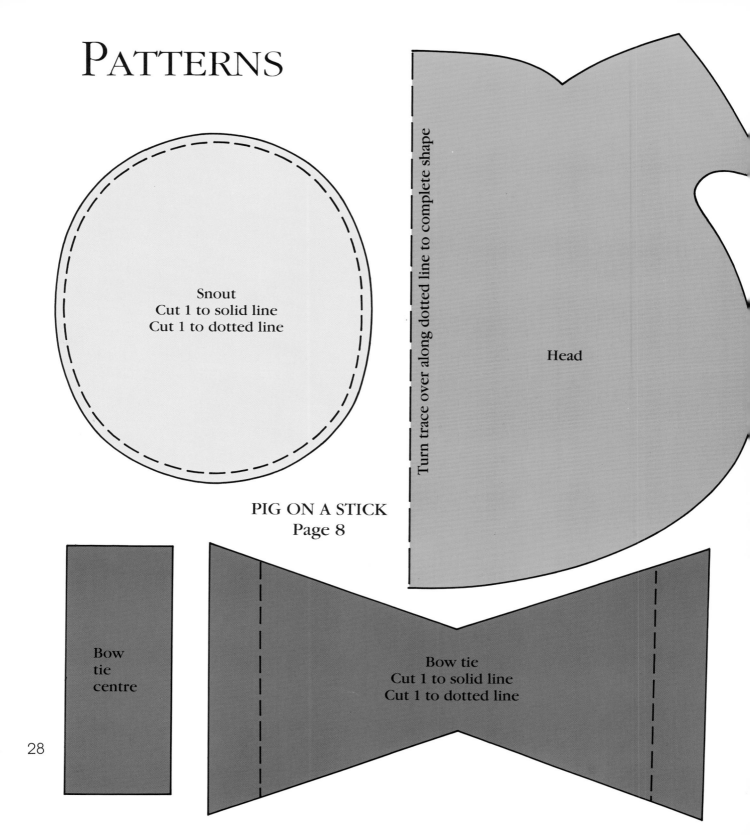

Snout
Cut 1 to solid line
Cut 1 to dotted line

Turn trace over along dotted line to complete shape

Head

PIG ON A STICK
Page 8

Bow
tie
centre

Bow tie
Cut 1 to solid line
Cut 1 to dotted line

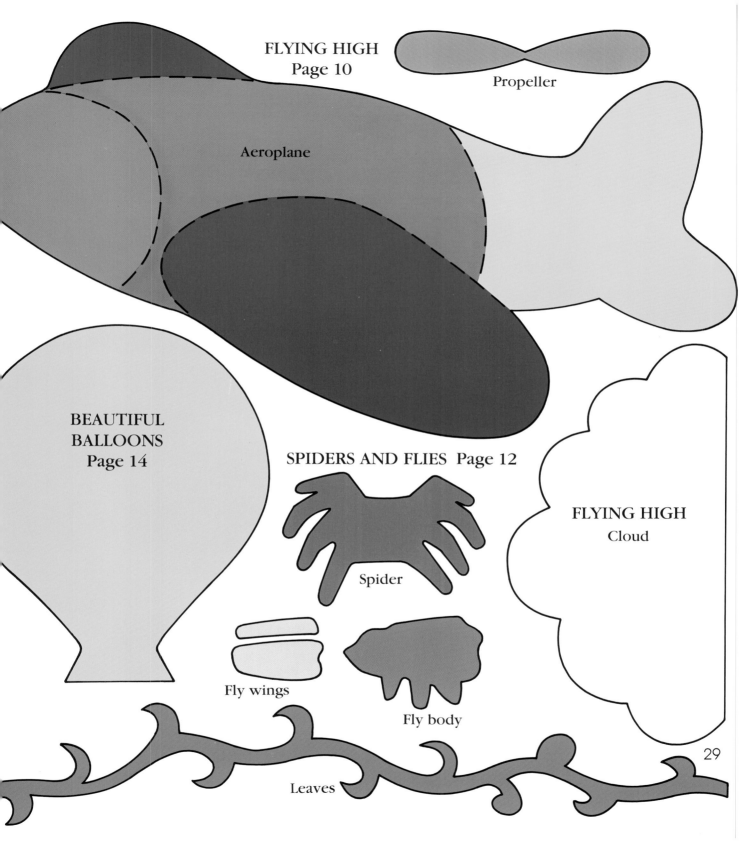

FLYING HIGH
Page 10

Propeller

Aeroplane

BEAUTIFUL
BALLOONS
Page 14

SPIDERS AND FLIES Page 12

Spider

FLYING HIGH
Cloud

Fly wings

Fly body

Leaves

29

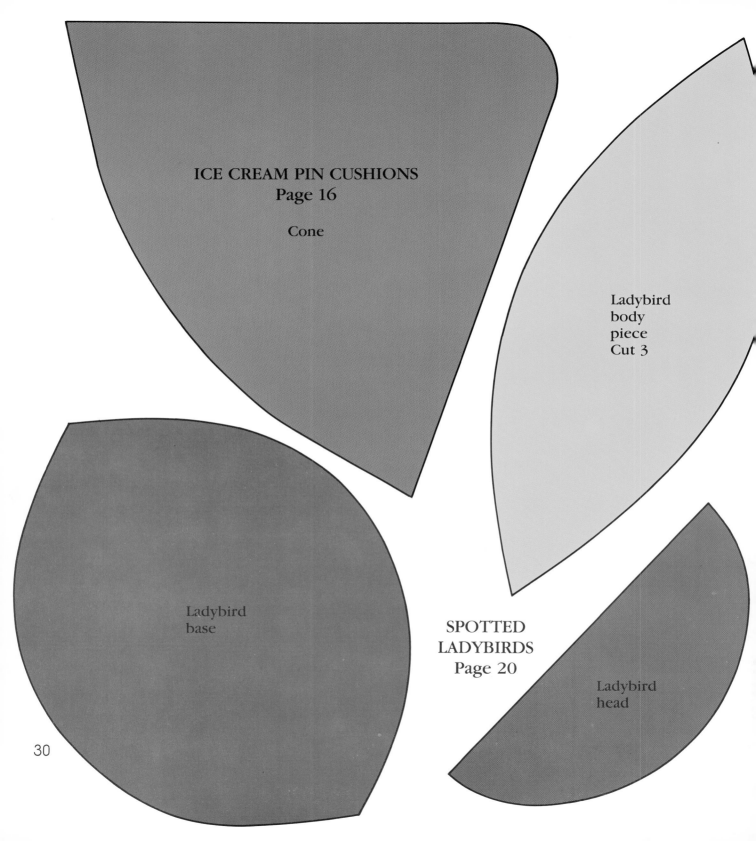

ICE CREAM PIN CUSHIONS
Page 16

Cone

Ladybird
body
piece
Cut 3

Ladybird
base

SPOTTED
LADYBIRDS
Page 20

Ladybird
head

30

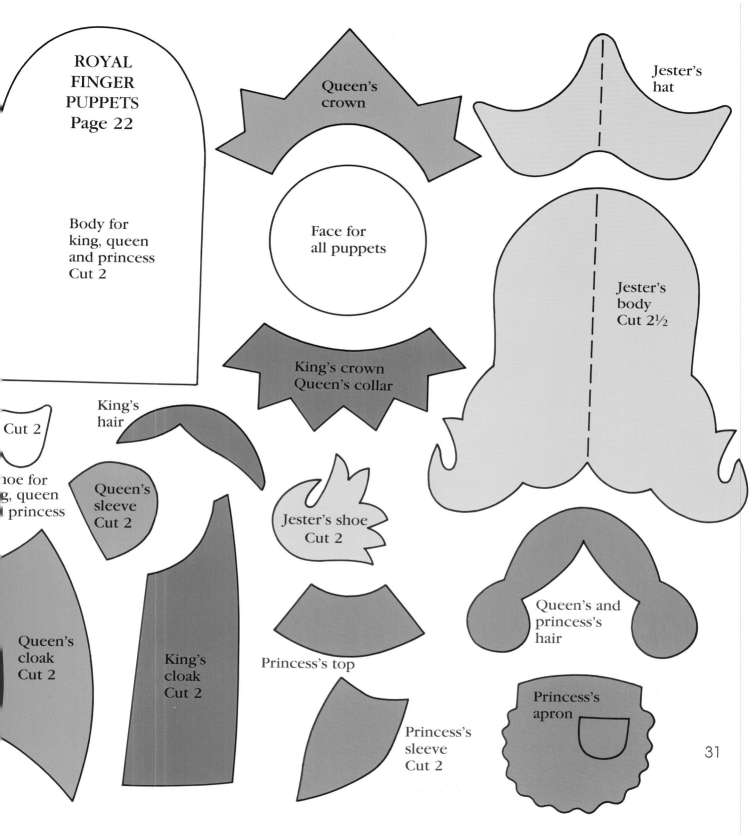

ROYAL
FINGER
PUPPETS
Page 22

Body for
king, queen
and princess
Cut 2

Queen's
crown

Jester's
hat

Face for
all puppets

Jester's
body
Cut 2½

King's crown
Queen's collar

Cut 2

King's
hair

oe for
g, queen
princess

Queen's
sleeve
Cut 2

Jester's shoe
Cut 2

Queen's and
princess's
hair

Queen's
cloak
Cut 2

King's
cloak
Cut 2

Princess's top

Princess's
apron

Princess's
sleeve
Cut 2

31

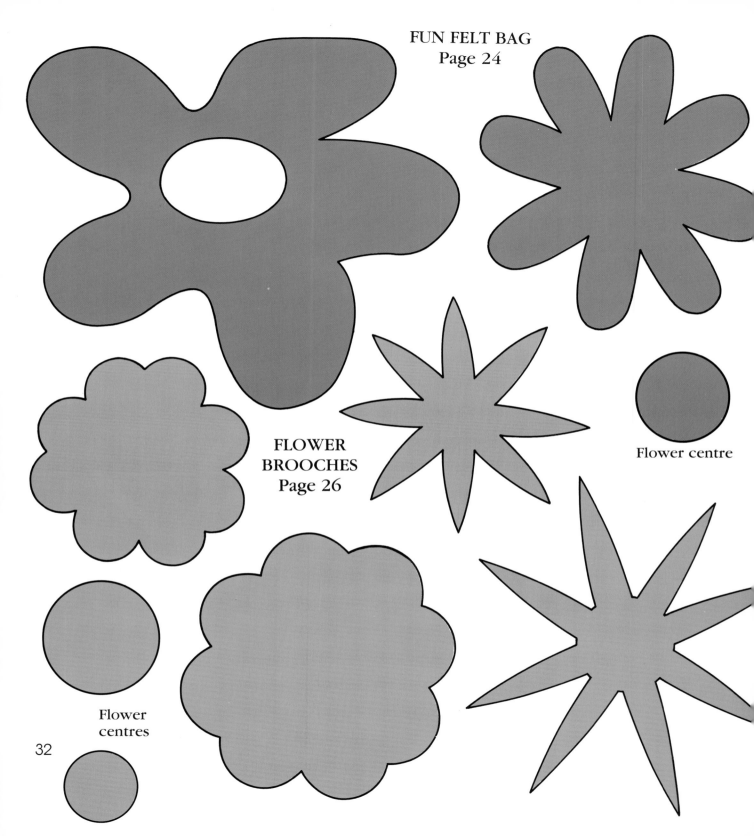

FUN FELT BAG
Page 24

Flower centre

FLOWER
BROOCHES
Page 26

Flower
centres

32